Do You Have the Rutter's Rudder?

A FAMILY HISTORY

Richard A. and Richard C. Newberg

ISBN: 978-1-0880-7242-4

Independently published in Little Rock, Arkansas.

J.H. Rutter

It is an ancient mariner,
And he stoppeth one of three...

Hello! My name is Andy Newberg, and I'm 51, and no, I'm not the Ancient Mariner. In fact, I don't even like the sea that much! I do have a tale to tell you that I'm sure you'll find interesting—if not, I'll buy you a steak dinner at the place of your choosing. Interested? This is a true story about the sea and it includes three generations of my personal family history going all the way back to my great-great grandfather, Andrew Newberg, who was born in Finland on December 3, 1850. As the story is somewhat lengthy, I'm only going to tell you the first part of the story, and my father, Richard, or "Newbs" as he likes to be called, will tell you the second, or last, part.

Let's start at the beginning by letting you know the cast of characters involved. My dad, Newbs, is the first. He and all my family reside in Little Rock, Arkansas, although he and my late mother, Honoré, both grew up and attended elementary and high school in Ludington, Michigan. How we all ended up in the Deep South, Little Rock, Arkansas, is another story for another day. Dad just recently turned 85 and finally retired this past July after pushing paper and preparing tax returns for 59 years. He now spends most of his time tying trout flies in his office behind the garage or chasing the illusive trout up on the Little Red River in Heber Springs, Arkansas.

Modesty is notone of my family's strong points, and Dad's

office walls are adorned with framed pictures of his many accomplishments, including his belonging to two separate Sports Hall of Fame organizations. He will quickly point out to you that he attended Kalamazoo College on a scholastic scholarship, played freshman basketball there, and walked onto the tennis team, which went 23-2 in 1955, and he, personally, was undefeated on what was considered the third best team in the country at the time. He subsequently transferred to the University of Mississippi on what may have been their first offered tennis scholarship and ended up playing number one during his senior year, 1961, albeit, he doesn't talk too much about his record there. He reluctantly admits, as does his doubles partner, Buddy, that all this took place before the Swedes arrived in the states and that both would probably now have a hard time even making the women's team.

Enough about Dad. What everyone notices when you enter his office is a framed oil painting of a large four-masted schooner called the *J. H. Rutter,* which is behind his desk and what this story is all about. On October 31, 1878, the *Rutter* appeared off Big Point Sable lifesaving station after having lost its rudder in a severe northwest storm. The vessel had encountered trouble while bound from Chicago, Illinois to Buffalo, New York with its cargo of 45,000 bushels of corn and 19,000 bushels of rye. The cargo had shifted, and the ship was listing dangerously to port. It was flying a distress signal in the form of the American flag flying upside down.

The western wind was all aflame,
The day was well-nigh done!

At that time, the Point Sable station was the only lifesaving station on the shore between Grand Haven, Michigan and Point Betsie. Its keeper, Capt. Sanford Morgan, was out of town in Detroit, but his son, James, was in charge of the crew and gave orders for them to assemble on the beach opposite the *Rutter*.

When they arrived on the beach, Capt. Simpson of the *J. H. Rutter* shouted to them that he needed a tug to tow his vessel to Ludington. The message was sent, and Capt. John Crawford turned his tug, the *Margaret,* over to Capt. Robert Caswell, Ludington's most experienced tugman. Sometime later, the *Margaret* arrived in company with the Goodrich steamer *DePere.*

Caswell had realized that the *Margaret* didn't have enough fuel to tow the *Rutter* all the way to Ludington. Instead, he proposed that the *DePere,* which happened to be in port, tow the schooner while the tug remained alongside with the lifesavers on board in case of trouble. This was soon agreed upon, and the trio of ships set out for Ludington.

After an extremely difficult trip from Point Sable with the *Rutter,* minus her helm and listing dangerously, the *DePere* and her tow arrived in Ludington. The *Rutter* dropped anchor off the spot where the Waterworks Station was located (Exhibit #2). The wind and the sea had gone down by that time, and the moon shone brightly. As they had done all that they could, the lifesaving crew went ashore and started overland to the Point.

Capt. Simpson sent word ashore that he wanted a number of men to shovel the grain back into place in the *Rutter*, offering $1 an hour for all who would volunteer their service. A crew of 40 men volunteered and was taken out in the *Margaret* to the *Rutter*. Among this group were George Harbaugh, John Hounsell, Sr., John Housel, Jr., and Andrew Newberg.

The *Margaret* tied up to the *Rutter*, so as to be on hand if needed, but at about 11:00 p.m., the wind came up and the sea rose so high that the motion of the boats parted the towline. The tug then could not lie there any longer, and Capt. Simpson made arrangements with Capt. Caswell that *the Margaret* should tie up inside the harbor entrance and, if any assistance was needed, a light would be hung on the forward rigging of the *Rutter* to summon help. Capt. Simpson then retired to his cabin for some much-needed rest, and *the Margaret* steamed away to the piers.

In the meantime, the 40 men from Ludington and four of the *Rutter*'s crew were working like mad, realigning the cargo of corn and rye. At about 2:00 a.m., someone discovered the hatch had washed away and water was pouring in the hold. The captain was summoned and, when he investigated conditions, found 13 feet of water in the hold and his ship sinking rapidly. Only a small lantern could be found aboard, the others having been broken before the *Rutter* reached Point Sable the previous day. This lantern was hung up in the shrouds as agreed upon, and, while waiting for assistance, Capt. Simpson ordered the anchors slipped that his ship might not sink in deep water. The boat lay with her bow pointing about southwest, and every wave washed over her decks. At the risk of being swept off at any moment, Andrew Newberg, John Hounsel and another unnamed sailor went forward over the slippery decks and cast off the anchor.

And the coming wind did roar more loud, And the sails did sigh like sedge:

The old wind blew a hurricane out of the caverns of the North, churning the icy waters of Lake Michigan over and about the ill-fated schooner. The poor souls who had hurriedly left their homes the night before to render assistance and maybe earn a few dollars little dreamed when they boarded the ship what experiences they were to encounter before leaving.

To save themselves from drowning in the icy waters, the men took to the rigging of the vessel. There they clung, with hearts anxiously awaiting assistance that did not come, for the rays of the little lantern were too feeble to penetrate far into the darkness where the *Margaret* lay safe and sound in the harbor.

The dawning of day disclosed the pathetic scene pictured in Dad's oil painting in his office. Some hundreds of people came from far and near who could only watch the spectacle with bated breath and were unable to render any assistance. With no lifesaving crew near, the lives of all the men seemed to be doomed.

At last, Disciple Abair started out with his team to bring the Point Sable lifesaving crew. It was a neverto-be-forgotten ride, with 45 lives at stake. He started at 7:00 a.m. and soon after 9:00 had the crew and apparatus on the grounds.

Three or four attempts were made to reach the sinking vessel with the life boat, but the seas were too heavy. Nine attempts to shoot a line out to the boat were made before a rope could be secured, but, even then, with the big seas rolling, nothing could be accomplished.

Capt. Amos Breinig and Capt. L. Sterling Sr., along with Capt. Caswell, all tug captains, wanted to take the government tug *Col. Graham* out to rescue the men. Their own boats were too large to ride safely over the bar but the *Graham* drew less water, and they knew she could make the trip without injury. But her master, Capt. Hendrick, would not go, nor would he let his boat go, until he had obtained permission from Washington, D.C.

When, at last, it did come, a scow was rigged up, and the lifeboat, with some members of the crew and several local fishermen and sailors, including one John Janette, was towed out to the *Rutter*. The sea was very high, and it was thought impossible for the tug to get alongside the *Rutter*. Capt. Louis Sterling, Duncan Dewar, and Judge S. D. Haight were on the scow, which was intended to be brought under *Rutter*'s broadside to transfer the stranded men from her to the scow, then let her drift ashore.

Under the keel nine fathoms deep,
From the land of mist and snow,

By the time this was established, it was nearly 3:00 p.m. The men on the *Rutter* had been up in the shrouds of the boat nearly 12 hours. They had witnessed the many futile attempts at rescue, and their hope for succor had been shattered often as the waves drove lifesavers back to shore along with the lines shot out to the boat that failed to reach them. They were well-nigh exhausted from the cold and exposure.

When the *Graham,* scow and the lifeboat arrived, the men had come down frozen from the *Rutter,* and it was a welcomed but difficult release for them.

The lifeboat pulled up to her, and John Hounsell, Jr., Mr. Wilson, George Harbbaugh, and four others were taken off first and brought in through the surf to the beach. The others boarded the scow and tug and came in at the piers.

As soon as the weather settled, much of the damaged grain was pumped out of the *Rutter's* hull, and she floated with scarcely any difficulty. After being fitted with a new rudder later, the craft was almost as good as ever (Exhibit #3).

The *Rutter,* 212 feet long with 38-foot beam and 14-foot depth, was built in Marine City, Michigan, in 1873. Formerly, she was a four-sticker, a type of craft now rarely seen, and was one of the largest boats of the early day fleet trading on Lake Michigan (Exhibit #4).

Capt. Kendrick received a first-class gold medal for his work on that memorable day, and James Cummings, engineer on the *Graham,* received a second-class medal. Kendrick continued to sail in government service until his death in Grand Haven, Michigan in 1918. Local sentiment was strongly in favor of giving Capt. Sterling some token of recognition of his services, but he never received any from the government, though the memory of his courage and daring will remain bright in the recollections of many local citizens.

Simpson never sailed again. He went to Kansas, where he was elected for three terms in Congress on the Populist ticket. He died in Wichita, Kansas in 1905.

The *J. H. Rutter* was salvaged and continued to sail the Great Lakes for another 20 years. In 1898, it was chartered for service in the coal trade between Newport News, Virginia, and New York City. Unfortunately, the *Rutter* collided on October 23, 1918 with the steamer *Texan* and shortly thereafter was sunk in the North River off Pier 20, New York City, according to a response my dad received from the Great Lakes Maritime Institution.

The harbor bay was clear as glass,
So smooth it was strewn!

Hello! I'm Andy's dad, Richard, but I prefer being called Newbs, and I will finish up the story. I'm 85 and close to being an Ancient Mariner! I'll even throw in a $40 dollar bottle of wine plus dessert if you don't find our story interesting. Andy, you did a great job, and, no, I don't have any suggestions or corrections. I will add a little bit more about me, naturally, and I'll relate what I learned about my great-grandfather, Andrew Newberg from Ancestry.com.

Andrew, as noted, was born in Finland in 1850 and came over to Ludington to do some carpentry work and, eventually, some fishing. He worked in lumber camps in Newago, Michigan. On his arrival in Ludington, he and several others built the sailing vessel *North Star*, of which he was the master and manager. He sailed the *North Star* for several years and then turned his attention to commercial fishing, which was a profitable operation for a vessel. In those days, local fishermen salted all catches and sold only salted fish. He, however, sold the first fresh fish out of Ludington and became a commercial fisherman. He sold the first shipment, consisting of 1,500 pounds of whitefish, to a Mr. Green in Milwaukee, Wisconsin. Later, he ran several types of boats in and out of Ludington. He also bought fruit in Ludington and shipped it to points on the Wisconsin shore. He had many exciting adventures and had the reputation of being willing to sail anything that would float. He and his wife, Katherine, celebrated their golden wedding anniversary in 1932—among the numerous gifts at the celebration was a bronze sheath of 50 golden roses from a friend in Detroit. He was 87 at the time of his death in 1937.

A little more about me seems appropriate. I've always been filled with too much pride, so upon graduation from high school and with no funds available for college, I went to work on the Great Lakes to provide for future college. Yes, I know I should have borrowed the money, but, like my dad, I've always hated to be indebted to anyone! As a result of my being so hard-headed I ended up spending three-plus years working instead of graduating from college in four years. I didn't finish college until June of 1961 but didn't have any debt upon graduation, and I had completed a six-month army tour of duty (Exhibit#11).

On my first day as a coal passer aboard the S. S. *Spartan*, I got sick to my stomach 21 times, but eventually I got my sea legs. I always hated working on the boats because you actually lived on them for 20 days and then were off for eight days. I spent the first nine months as a coal passer and, in subsequent years, was a dishwasher, pot-and-pan man, forward flicker (staterooms), deckhand, waiter, and eventually morning head waiter. All told, I've spent 23 months sailing Lake Michigan but still don't know how to sail. My good friend Buddy has a grandson, Jack, who sails in all kinds of tournaments, and I'm hoping he'll give me some instruction one of these days.

He prayeth best, who loveth best all things both great and small

The car ferries operated between Ludington, Michigan and Milwaukee, Manitowoc, and Kewanee, Wisconsin. I ended up working on four of their seven boats including the PM31 (City of Saginaw), S.S. *Spartan*, S.S. *Badger*, and the *City of Midland*. (Note—I never did work on the PM22 or the PM32 (City of Flint). I've also had an additional 21 other jobs in my life. My children never seem to remember this when I give them that old "money doesn't grow on trees" lecture.

Still with me? I'm nearing the end, and I've got a surprise ending coming up for you.

My wife surprised me with a thirty-day vacation in September to Destin, Florida. It was nice, but I'm just not a beach person. I did manage to read six books while sitting under a beach umbrella. I also enjoyed watching a couple dolphins play tag with three people in front of them on those things called paddleboards. My daughter Juli and her daughter came down to visit us for five days, which was fun. A day after our arrival, but before Juli and Cameron's arrival, we got hit by Hurricane Sally. Fortunately for us, we didn't even lose any power in our seven-story condo. The food in Destin is excellent, but we usually ordered takeout and wore our masks to avoid COVID-19.

Ten days after our Florida trip, Juli and Cameron took pity on me and drove the three of us up to Ludington for my second vacation. The fall colors were the best I've ever seen! Juli and Andy have their late mother's house on Lakeshore Drive right across from the lake. Being able to sip a little wine at 7:00 and watch the sun go down is an unbeatable combination. They need to hold onto it forever.

Now, for the rest of the story!

Epworth Heights Resort's entrance is only a mile to a mile and a half from Juli and Andy's house on Lakeshore Drive. It probably now has about 225 cottages, including one owned by my old doubles partner, Buddy. The resort now has a gatekeeper, and even I, who spent five wonderful summers working there as the tennis instructor back in the 60s, cannot enter without permission. The resort is on the lake, and my old friend Buddy's cottage is actually right on the water.

While tasting a dry cabernet with Juli on our next to last day in Ludington and watching the sun go down across the street on Lake Michigan, Juli tells me that her brother, Andy, and his wife, Miguel, are up in Ludington renting a cottage out at Epworth, like they have done in previous years. The cottage they have rented has a lot more room than the 900 square feet at Andy and Juli's 302 North Lakeshore Drive house, plus it has two bathrooms and television. Andy also emphatically mentions to Juli that there is "something" out at Epworth that I just have to see before I return on Saturday to Little Rock.

Alone, alone, all alone, alone on a wide, wide sea

I figure it's got to be something about tennis and where, or when, I won my first tennis tournament, beating Buddy in a long three-set final back in 1948. (Incidentally, I then won the tournament the next two years and retired the cup. I should probably have quit tennis right then.)

The next day we drive out to the resort but can't gain admittance, even though I tell the gatekeeper of my connection with Epworth. I can't reach Andy and reluctantly end up calling Buddy, back in Little Rock, on my cellphone. He, of course, agrees to let us in, and I hand the damn phone to the gatekeeper, who admittedly is just doing his job. We enter the sacred grounds of Epworth but can't find the object that Andy wants me to see. Juli drives us around for a while, and I do notice that someone has painted all the lines on the old tennis courts wrong. Courts I once ruled over for five years. Some of the courts even seem to have shrunk? Juli finally straightens me out by informing me that these are a new type of thing called Pickleball courts. Finally, just as we are about to get on the phone again with Andy to get more specific directions, we come upon a giant round boulder about four feet in diameter with the following words embedded upon it:

A TREASURE FROM THE PAST

FOUND ON THE BEACH OF EPWORTH SOUTH BEACH BETWEEN SANDY BANKS COTTAGE AND JOURNEY'S END COTTAGE DURING THE EARLY SPRING OF 1991. THIS OLD SHIP'S RUDDER WAS RECOGNIZED AS AN ARTIFACT FROM THE MARITIME HERIAGE OF THE GREAT LAKES. A TREASURE TO BE PRESERVED.

IT IS BELIEVED TO HAVE COME FROM A WRECKED SCHOONER OF THE 1860'S VINTAGE, AND IN VIEW OF ITS SURPRISINGLY WELL-PRESERVED CONDITION, MUST HAVE BEEN IN COLD WATER FOR MANY, MANY YEARS BEFORE IT REACHED THE BEACH OF EPWORTH.

THE RUDDER'S ORIGIN REPRESENTS THE OPINION OF A MARITIME ENTHUSIAST KNOWLEDGEABLE IN SUCH MATTERS OF EARLY SHIP DESIGN OF SCHOONERS ON THE GREAT LAKES DURING THAT PERIOD.

JUNE 8, 1991 LUDINGTON, MICHIGAN

From the fiends, that plague thee thus!— Why lookst thou so?"— "With my cross-bow I shot the Albatross."

And YES, reader, five feet from the boulder is an old wooden rudder, about 10 feet tall. Reader, do you have my story figured out yet? It's implying that all artifacts do *not* necessarily come from ships that are *sunken* in Lake Michigan (Exhibits #1 & 1A).

The first thing I did after picking myself up and getting my ass off the ground was to call Andy. I told him I had just *two* questions I wanted to ask him. He said, "fire away." I asked him if he could guess the present location of the schooner, *J. H. Rutter*, and the location of its rudder.

He said, "Dad, you and I know the *J. H. Rutter* is in New York, and it's been there off Pier 20 on the North River since 1918, and you are now probably looking at its rudder in Epworth and trying to figure how you and I can get a couple 2-foot-by-12-inch pieces off it, right?"

I don't raise any stupid children, do I?

Pentwater, Michigan is about 13 miles south of Ludington, and Charlevoix,, Michigan is about 142 miles north of

Ludington. Both cities are right on Lake Michigan, and both, unlike Ludington, have a nautical gift store catering to the tourists. They both sell jerseys, brass propellers, pennants, sextants, and artifacts, but the store in Charlevoix, Michigan also sells some furniture, like coffee tables. A typical tabletop might consist of three to four boards off an old wreck that have been planed down and sanded to perfection and include an imbedded brass plaque with an inscription such as, "Forward plank off the schooner *West Winds,* Sunk in storm off Charlevoix, November 11, 1 857."

"Dad, aside from us winning a Pulitzer Prize for our great story, how many of our three original requests do you really think we will obtain for all our hours of work that promote Epworth Heights Resort? You remember what we originally wanted, don't you—a piece of wood off the rudder to "insert" into our own individually-made coffee table, a new brass plaque honoring Andrew to be attached to the round boulder out at Epworth, and a lifetime pass in and out of Epworth?"

I thought for a minute and answered, "Two, or, no, probably just one. The idea about getting a pass won't happen. I just hope they make an audio version of our true story for my wife, Sandy, and one for our friend, Williamson, because they both don't read, you know."

Farewell, farewell! But this I tell
To thee, thou wedding guest!
He prayeth best, Who loveth best,
All things both great and small

"Look, Andy, I have an idea. I know I've already paid off our annual football bet on the Ole Miss/Arkansas football game, but I'll take us both to Scotty's for a steak dinner tonight, and we can share that excellent $40 bottle of wine I bought recently at the General Store in Petoskey, Michigan. You can spring for the dessert, all right? Over dinner we can decide who we want to produce our book: Grisham, who once lived in Oxford, Mississippi near my old campus at Ole Miss, or Patterson, who seems to be on the *New York Times* Bestseller list every damn week. Agreed?"

"Okay."

At length did come an albatross, Through the fog it came:

EXCERPTS FROM AN ARTICLE IN THE MARITIME HISTORY OF THE GREAT LAKES J. H. RUTTER (SCHOONER). U7 5504, DISABLED, 31 OCTOBER 1878

As a former practicing C.P.A., I'm well aware of copywriting and plagiarism, so I wish to point out here that the following well-written excerpts were not written by me but appeared in their publications above, and I'm including them only because I recently came across them and think they add even more drama to our story.

EXCERPT #1: (November 1, 1878, *Detroit Post and Tribune*):
The four mastered barge J. H. Rutter, of Toledo, is lying off Ludington, October 31, 1878 disabled. Her wheelhouse and gear are carried away. She has 6 feet of water in her hold, and her pumps have given out. She is said to be from Chicago, loaded with grain and rolling freight. The Life Savings Station at Point Au Sable has a crew and boat aboard of her now. The steamer DePere has been out all the afternoon trying to save her. The sea is running high, and it looks as if she must go on the beach.

EXCERPT#2: (November 2, 1878, *Detroit Post and Tribune*):
A day of thrilling excitement at Ludington.
(Special dispatch to the Post and Tribune.) Ludington, November 1, 1878.
(Received from our special correspondent):

When I got down to the shore this morning, the four mastered barge, John H. Rutter lay sunk a half mile north of the pier, and about the same distance from the shore, the sea rolling over her, and about 40 men, who went aboard of her of last evening to shovel grain, clinging to the rigging. The vessel had unexpectedly

GONE DOWN IN THE NIGHT,

And these men, wet and numb, clung to the masts. The lifeboat from Point au Sable was here and was manned by Capt. Sterling and a volunteer crew, but after two attempts, lasting two hours, it was found impossible to get the boat through the breakers. Not a tug in the harbor fit for such service would venture out, but Capt. Fred Kendrick, commanding a rickety tug owned by the government, offered to go and take the lifeboat through the breakers. It was about half-past eleven when the lifeboat was transported by wagon to the harbor. A scow was manned, and Capt. Kendrick started out of the harbor with the scow in tow. The lifeboat was manned by Capt. Simpson of the Rutter and some of his crew.

And now there came both mist and snow,
And it grew wondrous cold;

Hundreds upon hundreds watched the boat as they went out of the harbor and were taken in by hand by the waves. Occasionally neither tug, scow, nor lifeboat was visible. They

WERE THROWN ABOUT WITH TERRIFIC VIOLENCE,

but the little boat behind came out right side up every time. The attempt of the tug was to pull out to the windward and let the scow float alongside the vessel. While this was being done the crew from the Life Savings Station at Point Au Sable, which had meanwhile arrived, were using their mortar to shoot line over the vessel; but this was in vain. The mortar was too light. When a light cord was attached to the ball, it went almost to the vessel, but with a heavier one, it fell far short. Once the line broke and the ball passed over the vessel. For an hour seemingly the tug tried to get the scow alongside, but to no purpose, and hearts sunk she headed for the harbor. But then,

THE LIFEBOAT CUT LOOSE,

and succeeded in getting a line to the vessel and got alongside one after another of the sufferers jumped into her until seven were rescued. Then she started for the shore, drifting northwards. When she got within 40 rods of the shore the whole length of her line was out, and she could come no further without letting go the line. This she did and shot through the breakers like an arrow. Men ran into the surf and literally carried the boat up the bank.

It was now near two o'clock p.m., seven men saved and 33 on the wreck. The seven could scarcely walk. The wreck was

FAST GOING TO PIECES,

she was broken in the middle. Now came a long delay that was agonizing to the sufferers and to the thousands on shore. The lifeboat was again transported a mile back to the harbor by a wagon. They began the fourth attempt to save life. Capt. Morgan, with his life-saving crew started out through the piers in their lifeboat, this time with line enough. The waves

SWAMPED THE BOAT

in two minutes and drove it back on the shore north of the piers. The storm kept up. The wreck was breaking up and rolling about, and the sight of the of the sufferers out though the waves was a piteous appeal for help. None of the first-class tugs would face the storm. The lifeboat could not be got out through the breakers unless it was towed out. Fred Kendrick again volunteered with his old tug. Capt. Morgan manned his lifeboat and the ropes were got ready again. Just as the sun was going down, they started down past the pier for the fifth trial. The tug could be seen most of the time and the little boat behind was visible occasionally.

He holds him with his glittering eye—
The wedding guest stood still,

Several times it was

THROWN INTO THE AIR

apparently, and then engulfed. As they came into proximity with the wreck, the lifeboat was violently torn loose from the tug and driven towards shore. But Fred Kendrick would not give it up this time. Again and again, he tried to get to the wreck. A line went to frozen hands, and was made fast. Slowly she came near. Oh, what a rush. All were on the tug but one, the mate of the RUTTER. He cast off the line and fell rather jumped on the tug, the

LAST MAN TO LEAVE THE WRECK.

When the little tug got through the waves and rode into the harbor, cheer after cheer went up for Kendrick and for his crew, for Louis Sterling, Duncan Dewar, Billy Leet, and the brave men who volunteered to go.

She was in tow of the KETCHUM, but.was separated night before last in the storm. She showed distress signals yesterday off this port, and was brought to anchor near the shore by the DePere, and was supposed to be safe. She draws too much water to enter this harbor. George W. Barber, George Tracy, James Clark,

James Aury, Geo. Harbaugh, and Mero are the names of some who came near perishing—nearly all citizens of Ludington.

EXCERPT #3: (November 30, 1878, *Detroit Post and Tribune*):

The J. H. RUTER is in the harbor, lying on the bottom in 16 feet of water. The schooner GRACIE FILER, sailing into the harbor last night, stove in the RUTTER'S stern. As soon as her steering apparatus arrives, the RUTTER will be taken to Milwaukee.

Hi, readers! I must apologize for this double-*Carrie* movie-type ending to our story, but sometimes things just pop up that are hard to explain, and Andy and I were off to sip that $40 bottle of wine when we came across an article in the Maritime History of the Great Lakes. We acknowledge the excellent writing in the article and feel that we certainly need to include the three excerpts above in our story. Rather than going back and changing, modifying, or deleting and deep-sixing some of our work, have decided to show them here, at the end of what we thought was the end of our original story. Again, sorry, but, hell, we are not professional writers! Give us a break.

The very deep did rot: O Christ! That ever this should be!

Below are the stanzas of the 1927 poem by Michigan legislator, Hon. Virgil A. Fitch called "Sunset on the Stranded Rutter" (Exhibit #16):

Their names in bronze, lest we forget
Our own longshoremen true
Who left the harbor once to save
Brave "sockless Simpson's crew,

Young Harbaugh lived to tell the tale
Of how he reached the shore
Now Lake View children wonder why
"The white wings are no more,

"Twas in the fall of seventy-eight,
The harvest days were o'er:
To leisure bent in youthful joy
I lingered on the shore.

Toward the hungry East
From the prairies of the West
White-winged fleets were dancing
The skyline water's crest.

The raw and gusty weather
Had lasted many-a-day
And the sailors in distress
Were tacking for the bay

I saw a ship go down at sea
Off "Ludington-on-the-Lake"
It strewed its treasures on the deep
Like grain in the farmer's wake.

The raging sea was white with foam
For miles outside the strand
And combing billows came to shore
And crept far up the land.

And a good south wind sprung up behind
The albatross did follow

The angry waters leaped on high
The winds bore down the main
At sixty miles an hour or more
It was a hurricane.

The ship had lost its rudder
And had listed in a trough
When two-score volunteers steamed out
To throw the cargo off.

Captain Caswell with his tug
No stouter heart than he
Convoyed the workers to the ship
Careening in the sea.

Then the moon went down
And the storm witch squalled
And landward and seaward
The for-horn called

Till an eagle saw
In its piney nest
Dim lights go out
In the inky West

All through the watch with Newberg
The valiant crew had worked
The waves had washed the mizzen shrouds
But not a man had shirked.

When lo! A cry, "we're sinking"
Went ringing thought the craft
Then sea nymphs danced upon the decks
And chattering sylvan laughed.

The fair breezed blew, the white form flew
The furrow follow'd free,

The mate had called for volunteers
To close the hatch below;
Jack Hounsel and his fearless sire
But ran the overflow

"Twas Captain Jerry Simpson
Who manned the fated craft;
Good "sockless Jerry Simson,"
The bravest man afloat.

"Tis true he went to Congress
To command a "ship of state,"
But the way he manned the "Rutter'
Made him already great.

He cheered the boys in the rigging
As his barge sank in the wave,
And the morning found them clinging
Above a watery grave.

There were boys out in the rigging
And mothers on the shore,
And God was in his Heavens
Above the tempest's roar.

How well do I remember
That time and time again
Lines were shot from booming mortar
Falling short upon the main.

How lifeboats manned with sailors true
Were thrown back on the sand,
"Till it seemed as if the sea gods
Were fighting with the land.

How the heart fought with the water
"Till the billows found a foe
That will live in future story
As long as the seas do flow.

How on that awful sunset,
When the city was in despair
A judge (Judge Haight) who looked thru nature
Planned a fleet to go out there

To the capital of the Nation
The starling news had sped.
"Take out the tug brave Kendrick,"
A lightning message said.

"Throw me a line," spoke Sterling,
"With the Judge and Doc and Dewar
I'll lash a scow on the lee of the wreck
And make the chances sure."

How that tug flew out the harbor,
Moving like a thing of life,
Towing a scow and lifeboat
Out through the water's strife

Young Morgan's at the helm on the lifeboat,
McFay has the oar near the prow,
Costello's with Kendrick and Cummings,
Me-thinks I see them now,

Rising in the golden sunset,
Sinking as if for breath,
Living again by the sunken ship
To rob the wreck of death.

No pageant of the ocean grand
No deed where armies meet
On the land or in the Navy
Out-glows that gallant feat.

For a golden sun in a silver sea
Throws a halo o'er the spray,
Glorifying all the sailors
On the Lakes and in the Bay,

Then hurrah for the galiant tug
For the hearts in the lifeboat too,
Braving old Neptune's yawning teeth
To rescue the "Rutter's" crew.

For Sterling, Dewar, Shorts, and Haight
Silhouetted against the sky,
Enshrined heroes of that day,
Your deeds will never die.

Great steamships ply and go
And "white wings" are no more,
For the sailor of ye' olden time
Is on the farther shore.

We drifted o'er the harbor bar,
And I with sobs did pray—

Sandy, do you now realize why it was so important for me to finish that task I was working on by the first of November? November 1, 2020, is the 142nd-year anniversary of the *Rutter*'s battle with nature that took place November 1, 1878. Andy and I both honor and appreciate what Andrew Newberg and the crew, sailors and townspeople of Ludington accomplished to save the *John H. Rutter* back on November 1, 1878.

Andy and I are now through with this story for the second time, and yes, we again are off to Scotty's to finish that wine with a good steak:

Richard Charles Newberg ("Newbs")

11-1-2020

Richard Andrew Newberg ("Andy")

11-1-2020

He holds him with his skinny hand,
"There was a ship," quoth he.

KATHERINE NEWBERG, "AUNT KITTY":

Reader—I know, I've punished you enough for one evening, and I also promised I'd end this story on page number 13, but I got to thinking and would be remiss if I failed to give you a little information about two people who are extremely interconnected with the story. Why don't you fix yourself a toddy, and I'll hurry and finish up, okay? First, let me tell you about my late great-aunt, Katherine, "Aunt Kitty," the daughter of Andrew, the hero and person this story is all about. Aunt Kitty gave me whatever pride and gumption I have in life. She graduated from the University of Michigan with honors and never let anyone forget it! I graduated tenth in my high school class of one hundred twenty-seven and upon graduation received an ego-boosting letter from the University of Michigan acknowledging that I would be accepted if I so chose to attend their fine school. I'm sure that Kitty had written to the university on my behalf (Exhibit #10).

Upon graduation, she went to work as a school teacher in Ypsilanti, Michigan. In those days, 1909, women didn't live by themselves, and she had to live with the mayor and his wife while teaching school. She eventually ended up in my hometown, Ludington, and taught French at my high school. Kitty never married, and rumor has it that she had one brokenhearted love affair in her life.

I've always tried to respect my elders and frequently took both of my children with me when I went to visit her in her large two-story home where she lived all by herself. On one particular visit, I remember saying in front of her, and my children, that I grew up without watching television and that all we had back then to entertain ourselves with was radio and Jack Benny and Bob Hope. Kitty's response was priceless. "Yes, I remember when we got the radio."

Another thing I will always remember is the actual visits themselves. We would usually find her working in her garden attacking any weeds foolish enough to being life there. She warmly invited us in and offered up coke to Andy and Juli and left over strong, iced tea to me. We always seemed to end up in the living room, which I called the "purple room" as it seemed to blend with the healthy African Violets she constantly grew. I, of course spent most of my time looking at portrait of the J. H. Rutter in the center of living room wall while Kitty quizzed the kids about what they were reading or doing during their summer months and hoped that they were visiting the local library.

I like to fish and for about a twelve-year period got into salmon fishing. Trying to catch and release a salmon is an amazing thing—it took me two years to even land my first one. Hooking a salmon is, in itself, a difficult task. These fish that come up the Pere Marquette River near Baldwin, Michigan, are there to spawn, not feed, and you can spend hours throwing your hand-tied flies at them with no response. After a few years, I learned a thing or two, but playing an 8-to-20-pound salmon on a fly rod is a lot of fun but isn't easy. I eventually had to beach them because I didn't have any help in landing them, as I was usually fishing alone and couldn't get the fish close enough for to me to use my long, beautifully-handmade wooden net.

Aunt Kitty's birthday fell on October first every year which coincided with the opening day of salmon fishing. I recall, after the end of a day's fishing, picking and bringing her a dozen wildflowers. At that time, she was living in an assisted living home about 8 miles east of Ludington, and how her eyes did shine. At age 90, she had finally fallen in her old two-story home because she wouldn't sleep downstairs in the room where her parents had slept. My aunt, Alice, then finally convinced her to move to a very nice assisted living home.

And now the storm—blast came, and he Was tyrannous and strong:

Every year when I returned to chase the salmon, my fishing buddies would kid me and ask if I was up from Little Rock for my great-aunt's birthday, not realizing she was still alive and that I actually looked forward to visiting her. They even did this the same day she turned 100! Aunt Alice, once a teacher herself, looked after her and visited Kitty frequently. Alice had asked, and I had agreed, to picking Kitty up and taking her the eight-mile trip to the Ludington Community Church. I never dreamed that this was going to be a big celebration. I was dressed in my fishing clothes and picked Kitty up at noon. For some unknown, unfathomable reason, I failed to realize that living to be a 100 is a BIG DEAL!

I arrived where Kitty was living, and she was ready and nicely dressed. On the way to the church, we talked and she fussed a little about my driving and noticed all the construction taking place. She was razor-sharp regarding anything a few years back and quizzed me about my wife, Sandy, and how she was doing and how many pupils she had to manage in her teaching position back in Little Rock, Arkansas

The church was filled with people including a state senator and a state representative. I was embarrassed about my clothing and tried to say as little as possible. I actually sort of hid myself as much as possible behind a plate of chocolate cake.

The one thing I'll always remember about that day, after I carefully got her out of my car back at the assisted living home, still rings vividly in my ears. I said, "Aunt Kitty, I bet you are a little tired?" She replied, "Yes, Dickey, but it's a good kind of tired!" Incidentally, Aunt Kitty is the only person who ever called me "Dickey" and got away with it. She actually made it another year to 101 but then faded fast.

PADEN CHRISMAN:

One last person to talk about, and like Samuel Taylor Coleridge's wedding guest, I promise I'll let you go. This person is another great fisherman, Paden, the son of Juli and her husband Tracy (and my grandson). And yes, he's the great-great-great-grandson of Andrew Newberg, who I'm sure, would welcome him aboard any boat he sailed as first mate. I got Paden hooked on fishing at age four, and I firmly believe that he now has passed me by. When Paden was six, he accomplished the hat trick, which earned him a hat with that notation on it. It denotes catching on the same day, a Rainbow, Brown and Brook trout. At age 10, his mother turned him loose during the summer months in Ludington and let him ride his bike down to the local marina, where one day he hooked into a good-sized salmon.

He was fishing by himself off a little dock and knew he would lose the fish if he tried to lift it that extra 3 yards to where he was sitting. He solved the problem and caught the fish by jumping off into the water, which was only about 3 feet deep, and somehow throwing the fish up onshore. An observer paid him $10 for the salmon (Exhibit#13).

Upon the whirl, where sank the ship,
The boat spun round and round;

Paden is now a 6-foot-5, 19-year-old sophomore at Mississippi State College, Starkville, Mississippi. His major course of study, as you can probably guess, is Wildlife, Fisheries and Aquaculture. I'm biased, of course, but he is one of the best fishermen I've ever been around. Arkansas is fortunate in having many excellent places to fish. There, for children "under 16 years of age" and for "handicapped people," like yours truly, is an area called Dry Run Creek, next to the hatchery in Mountain Home, Arkansas. It is a designated "no-kill" fishing zone loaded with giant brown and rainbow trout. I once watched Paden catch and release 32 trout, most of which were in the 17-to-24-inch class.

Paden told me once that he had caught a small shark, a stingray, a redfish and a sheepshead. Two years ago, for the first time ever, the four of us managed to get off from work and school at the same time... We all went up to Ludington in October to do a little salmon fishing. Paden has played and caught so many big fish that I knew he would love playing the 8-to-20-pound salmon. I informed him before we left for our trip that during my twelve years chasing these monsters, years ago, that, after not landing a salmon during my first two years, I eventually learned a thing or two. I was usually fishing by myself and just about always had to beach my fish, or drag them out of the water up onto shore, due to their weight. I casually mentioned that on my best day fishing for them I had actually landed or beached four!

I hate telling you this, but on Paden's second day of salmon fishing, he also caught four big salmon. Not only did he do this but he tailed all four, by getting them fairly close to where he was playing the fish, and then reaching down into the water with his bare hand, not the casting or hand being used to fight the fish, and simply lifting the fish out of the water by the tail.

As my wife and Paden's mother, Juli, say, I have created a monster (Exhibit #15).

Exhibits for J. H. Rutter

1A. Picture of *J. H. Rutter*'s rudder and stone with embedded memorial plaque

1. Description of embedded inscription on plaque regarding *J. H. Rutter,* located at Epworth Resort, Ludington, Michigan

2. Explanation of where Water Works Park is located & its relevance to *J. H. Rutter*

3. Copy of picture of wrecked *J. H. Rutter*

4. Copy of who built *J. H. Rutter,* but as yet, inadvertently unconfirmed

5. Copy of email to Tim Colton, requesting revision in accordance with an article in Maritime History of the Great Lakes

6. Copy of webpage listing the *J. H. Rutter*'s operation on Lake Michigan, builder, and date of building

7. Copy of my November 21, 1990 letter to Great Lakes Maritime Institution with notation of its finally being sunk in

North River, New York on October 23, 1918 after a collision with steamer *Texan*

8. Copy of unanswered request about the tugboat *Margaret*

9. Photo of Ludington's lighthouse off North Pier

10. Copies of obituaries of Andrew Newberg and his daughter Katherine, "Aunt Kitty"

11. Richard C. Newberg and I's job experience (2 pages)

12. My son and I's Ancestry chart (3 pages)

13. Fish caught by Paden (3 pages)

14. Family photo of Andrew Newberg, born December 3, 1850

15. Photo of Paden

Picture of *J. H. Rutter*'s rudder and stone with embedded memorial plaque

Exhibit 1A

Description of embedded inscription on plaque regarding *J. H. Rutter,* located at Epworth Resort, Ludington, Michigan

Exhibit 1

WATER WORKS, LUDINGTON, MICHIGAN

The "Water Works", as mentioned in our "Rutter Novel", is a picnic area at the furthermost Western place on Tinkham Avenue, in Ludington, Michigan. It is where I, my parents, cousins and grandparents use to go for a relaxing "get together" & share some great food when I was a10-15 year old boy growing up in a wonderful town.

If you travel about 50 yards west of the picnic area you run into and enter Lake Michigan. This location is not more than one to two miles South from where the supposedly "unidentified " rudder" was found between the "Sandy Banks Cottage" and the "Journey's End" cottages out at Epworth Resort.

Explanation of where Water Works Park is located & its relevance to *J. H. Rutter*

Exhibit 2

Copy of picture of wrecked *J. H. Rutter*

Exhibit 3

Morley & Hill, Marine City MI

Most recent update: May 6, 2016.

William B. Morley and John J. Hill started this yard in 1869. If anyone can tell me more, or add to the table below, please send your info to timcolton@aol.com

Hull #	O.N.	Original Name	Original Owner	Type	GT	Built	Disposition
		C. N. Johnson					
	6767	D. W. Powers		Cargo Ship	303	1871	George W. Johnson 1893, Emerald 1898, abandoned 1910
	67128	Northerner	J. M. Nicol	Barge	1,214	1871	Cargo ship 1880, burnt and sank 1892 in L'Anse MI
	110043	Robert Holland		Cargo Ship	340	1872	Northern Queen (Canada) 1878, Robert Holland 1882, burnt 1915 in Sturgeon Bay
		Garvis Lord	?				
	90524	Minneapolis		Cargo Ship	1,072	1873	Foundered 1894 in Straits of Mackinaw
		Abercorn	?				
	130033	N. K. Fairbank		Cargo Ship	980	1874	Eliza H. Strong 1899, burnt and sank 1904 off Lexington Harbor
	125408	City of New Baltimore		Cargo Ship	80	1875	Abandoned 1916
	91129	Morley	J. J. Morley	Cargo Ship	869	1879	Grand Traverse 1887, in collision and sank 1896 near Colchester Light
	105937	A. L. Hopkins	J. J. Morley	Cargo Ship	756	1880	Foundered 1911 off Ontonagon MI
		J. Macy					
	76307	J. M. Osborne		Cargo Ship	646	1882	In collision and sank 1884 off Whitefish Point
	91493	Mary	C. & E. McElroy	Cargo Ship	117	1882	Burnt 1908 in Chelsea MA
	130333	New Orleans		Cargo Ship	1,457	1885	In collision and sank 1906 in Thunder Bay
	140882	Louisiana	W. B. Morley	Cargo Ship	1,753	1887	Wrecked and burnt 1913 Washington I
	81191	William B. Morley	Morley & Hill	Cargo Ship	1,846	1888	Caledonia 1889, Gale Staples (Canada ON 134518) 1916, wrecked 1918 near Au Sable Point Light
	100450	Italia	W. C. Morley	Cargo Ship	2,036	1889	Barge 1915, scuttled 1920 in Lake Erie
	77002	John J. Hill	C. T. Morley	Cargo Ship	974	1892	Burnt and sank 1908 off Frying Pan Shoal
	81391	W. B. Morley	Morley & Hill	Cargo Ship	1,748	1892	Scrapped 1923
	115784	Silvanus J. Macy	Peninsular Tpn	Cargo Ship	752	1881	Foundered 1902 off Port Burwell
	116331	St. Lawrence	C. T. Morley	Cargo Ship	1,437	1890	Wrecked 1898 off Point Betsie

Copy of who built *J. H. Rutter*, but as yet, inadvertently unconfirmed

Exhibit 4

2/2020 Possible addition to Morley & Hill, Marine City, MI listing of ships (supposedly built in 1873)

Subject: **Possible addition to Morley & Hill, Marine City, MI listing of ships (supposedly built in 1873)**

Date: 10/21/2020 3:58:24 PM Central Standard Time

From: newbergr@aol.com

To: timcolton@aol.com

Tim:

I have & can forward to you an excerpt from the Maritime History of the Great Lakes about the J. H. Rutter (Schooner), U75504, disabled 10-31-1878. My great grandfather, Andrew Newberg,actually went aboard the slippery decks of the ship during a violent storm to help cast off the anchor.After the storm subsided the damaged grain aboard was pumped off the hull and she was refloated and outfitted with a new rudder & put back into use.After being salvaged she continued to sail the Great Lakes for another 20 years. In 1898 it was chartered for service in the coal trade between Newport News, VA and New York City.Unfortunately the Rutter collided 10-23-18 with the steamer Texan and was sunk in the North River off Pier 20, N. Y. City , according to a 1990 response I received from the Great Lakes Maritime Institution.

Richard C. Newberg, CPA

Copy of email to Tim Colton, requesting revision in accordance with an article in Maritime History of the Great Lakes

Exhibit 5

MARITIME HISTORY
OF THE GREAT LAKES

Search (Advanced) → What's New → Details → 108 and 109

Search Site [ ] Go

R. L. Polk & Co.'s Marine Directory of the Great Lakes... 1888, 108 and 109

Pages [Select] Search within this title

PDF version of the page

ALPHABETICAL LIST OF VESSELS ON THE GREAT

Name.	Rig.	Tonnage.	Where Built.	By Whom.	When Built.	
		Tonnage	When Built	By whom	When Built	
[illegible]	Prop.	[illegible]	[illegible]	[illegible]	[illegible]	[illegible]
[illegible]	Barge	[illegible]	[illegible]	A. Miller	[illegible]	[illegible]
[illegible] David W	Prop.	[illegible]	Saginaw	Arnold	[illegible]	[illegible]
[illegible]	Prop.	15	Philadelphia	Neafie & Levy	[illegible]	[illegible]
[illegible]	Schr.	[illegible]	Port Dalhousie	S. Andrews	[illegible]	[illegible]
Rutter → Rutter J H	Barge	[illegible]	Marine City	Lester	[illegible]	[illegible]
[illegible]	Schr.	112	Kingston		[illegible]	[illegible]
[illegible]	Tug	14	Lockport		[illegible]	[illegible]

Search (Advanced) → What's New → Details → 108 and 109

The Maritime History of the Great Lakes site is managed by Walter Lewis
Since 2005 this site has been the prototype for the digital collection management tools built for the Our Digital World (formerly the OurOntario project of Knowledge Ontario.)
As a prototype it is subject to occasional, unexplained interruptions in service ... because we keep trying new things.

Powered by / Alimenté par vita digital toolkit

Copy of webpage listing the *J. H. Rutter*'s operation on Lake Michigan, builder, and date of building

Exhibit 6

RICHARD C. NEWBERG
CERTIFIED PUBLIC ACCOUNTANT
6219 CANTRELL ROAD
LITTLE ROCK, ARKANSAS 72207

MEMBER AMERICAN INSTITUTE OF CERTIFIED PUBLIC ACCOUNTANTS

TELEPHONE 501-663-8257

November 21, 1990

Mrs. Kathleen McGraw
c/o Great Lakes Maritime Institution
Dossin Museum 313 267 6440
Strand Drive, Belle Isle
Detroit, Michigan 48207

Atlant[ic]
coal 1898
sunk - Texan 1918
steamer
10-23 Pier 20, N.Y. City
North River N.Y. City

Dear Mrs McGraw:

I'm interested in the final resting place of the schooner, J. H. Rutter, on which my great grandfather once voluntarily performed some rescue work.

Enclosed is a short article describing the vessel.

I have enclosed a self-addressed postcard for your convenience or you could call me collect if you have any information as to the vessel's whereabouts.

Your help is most appreciated.

Very truly yours,
Richard C. Newberg

(12-7-90 con[versation] ... Dossin Museum)

Enclosure (— JH Rutter moved to Atlantic Coast in 1898 for coal traffic. Collided with steamer Texan & sunk in North River 10-23-1918 off Pier 20, N.Y. City (heavy traffic area - probably eventually dismantled.?)

Exhibit #7

Copy of my November 21, 1990 letter to Great Lakes Maritime Institution with notation of its finally being sunk in

Exhibit 7

RICHARD C. NEWBERG
CERTIFIED PUBLIC ACCOUNTANT
6219 Cantrell Road
Little Rock, Arkansas 72207

MEMBER AMERICAN INSTITUTE OF CERTIFIED PUBLIC ACCOUNTANTS
FAX 501-614-6392
TELEPHONE 501-663-8257
E-mail Newbergr@AOL.COM

February 22, 2008

(No Response!)

Mr. David Petersen
History Columnist
Ludington Daily News
North Rath Avenue
Ludington, MI 49431

Dear David:

I'm a transplanted Ludington native who use to live right across the street from the News & enjoy reading your column & seeing old pictures of my "old" home town.

I'm hoping you can help me with the whereabouts of a tugboat, named the "Margaret", as mentioned in the enclosed article. As noted in the article my great-grandfather, Andrew Newberg, helped during a daring 1878 rescue of the wrecked schooner, J. H. Rutter.

Unfortunately, I found out, via the Michigan Maritime Association, that the J. H. Rutter was eventually scuttled in the East River of New York, so, next best thing, is the Margaret. My late great Aunt, Katherine Newberg (lived to be 101), willed to me a beautiful oil painting of the foundering Rutter & it hangs in my office. As you can probably guess, I'd pay dearly to get a plank, or two, off the old tug Margaret.

Must get back to preparing a few tax returns but help me out if possible. Also, keep up the "good" work-enjoyed your pictures & article about the State Park Dam.

Very truly yours,

Richard C. Newberg
Enclosure

Copy of unanswered request about the tugboat *Margaret*

Exhibit 8

Photo of Ludington's lighthouse off North Pier

Exhibit 9

Katherine E. Newberg

BORN
OCTOBER 1, 1889

—

DIED
NOVEMBER 14, 1990

—

SERVICES FROM
THE COMMUNITY CHURCH
LUDINGTON, MICHIGAN
11:00 A.M. — NOVEMBER 17, 1990

—

OFFICIATING
REV. WILLIAM COLLINS

—

FAMILY
SISTER-IN-LAW - MARTHA NEWBERG
NIECES - ALICE MEISENHEIMER,
BEVERLY KENNEDY, JOYCE MORRISON
PEGGY SCOTT, CAROLYN SONGER,
MARTHA JANE BATSCHE
NEPHEWS - DONALD, ROBERT
AND PHILLIP NEWBERG

—

INTERMENT
LAKEVIEW CEMETERY
LUDINGTON, MICHIGAN

—

ARRANGEMENTS BY
ALEXANDER-RYE FUNERAL HOME
LUDINGTON, MICHIGAN

[illegible]

ANDREW NEWBERG DIES EARLY TODAY

Sturdy Pioneer Was First to Ship Fresh Fish From Ludington

[illegible]

Copies of obituaries of Andrew Newberg and his daughter Katherine, "Aunt Kitty"

Exhibit 10

JOB EXPERIENCE-RICHARD C. NEWBERG (My Docs #2)

1945-2020

1. Hasson Transfer Company-(First job-only worked couple days a week for friend of my father's-helped move Sears Catalogs, appliances & refrigerators)
2. Mini Newberg, grandmother(-Picked cherries & had to get up at t 5:30 a. m.- learned that an 8 yr. old Mexican boy could pick 3 times more cherries than I could during a 4 hour period)
3. Ludington Daily News-(Pedaled/delivered about 85 papers to North side of Epworth Hts. Resort, about 3 miles outside of town. Could finish this job in 45 minutes in order to play tennis)
4. Ludington State Fair-(Worked one of the concession stands. My father finally convinced me to ask what was my hourly rate of pay. Upon discovering how low it was I wisely quit!)
5. Self-employed-(Sold hot dogs at the beach on the 4th of July but didn't know how much I made. Learned that "bookkeeping" is an essential part of every job)
6. Extra jobs-(Cut grass & even painted window sill of local barber shop-must've cut 20 lawns to earn money for a $8.65 "Joe Gordon" baseball glove. Note-father then stepped in & paid off about 25% of balance)
7. Bonsers Grocery-(Stocking clerk-once plucked feathers off scalded, dead chickens)
8. J C Penney-Clerk-(Part time salesman & stock boy, on Saturdays in high school (Although never entrusted entirely with customer money which had to be pneumatically dispatched upstairs)
9. Chesapeake & Ohio Car Ferries;
10. 1. Coal passer- for 13 months (threw up 21 times first day)
11. 2. Pot & Pan man-(Necessitated a shower @ end of shift to eliminate kitchen odors)
12. 3. Dish washer-(Necessitated a shower @ end of shift to eliminate kitchen odors)
13. 4. "Forward Flicker"-(Cleaned & made up state rooms of passengers)
14. 5. Deck hand-(Helped tie up ship when docking during winter months)
15. 6. Waiter & eventually "Morning Head Waiter"-(Good pay & great tips)
16. Chesapeake & Ohio Railway-(Section hand laying rail and moving/installing railroad ties, worked with 5 blacks & 4 Mexicans, on "road" gang. They use to let me & another 16 yr. old Mexican try to lay track @ end of day while they all laughed their heads off! The blacks, who were nice, called me "School boy!)
17. Pentwater Wire Company-(Filled wooden jigs with wire & welded pieces together to form baskets, -Sparks caused burns on wrists)
18. City of Ludington-(Took the dog census with 3 other guys I'd hired and got paid .10 per dog after asking owner if dogs were male, female or spayed.)
19. Stokely Van Camp-(Ran bean canning machine & one day turned out over 99,999 cans of beans!)
20. Epworth Hts. Resort, before season opened-(Swept sand off walks-met Ginny Ledbetter one fine morning
21. Epworth Hts. Resort-Dining room-(Washing dishes again, for what was supposed to be only four hours, but always ended up being 5 or 6! Worked 3 days and then quit)
22. Phillips Service Station, Oxford, MS-(Ran convenience store/gas station for the father of a tennis teammate. Pumped gas & learned from a black customer that "coal oil" means "Kerosene"! Also changed flat tires using only a tool bar!)
23. Epworth Hts. Resort-Tennis Pro-(Giving lessons , stringing rackets, equipment sales, running annual guest tournament (made over $2,500 one year-wonder if they still might hire me?)
24. Dow Chemical Company-(Maintenance-helped clean giant chemical tanks while wearing a yellow rubber water proof suit. Days were long & cold!)

Richard C. Newberg and I's job experience

Exhibit 11 (1 of 2)

25. U. S. Post Office--(Christmas temporary work-helped with parcel post delivery & ended up drinking about a dozen "hot chocolates & 2 dozen cookies per day from holiday happy postal recipients)
26. Cotham, Wyman & Howland CPA's-(10years senior accountant & became the fastest ten key operator on adding machines in Arkansas. Had the best boss ever!)
27. Diversified Financial Services-(10 years as controller, in charge of back office-held positions as Secretary-Treasurer, holding security licenses with NASD/SEC & a real estate license with the Arkansas Real Estate Commission, as licensed realtor and also an insurance license- had second worst boss ever!)
28. Madigan & Company-(Senior accountant performing audits & reviewing work of junior accountants. Worst boss ever!)
29. Richard C. Newberg, CPA-CPA-(Specializing in tax preparation. My original goal was to make my CPA firm as big, or bigger, than the international firm, Arthur Anderson CPA's. Low and behold, I Did!
30. Retired 7-15-2020

Note:
All the above jobs helped mold me into "great" man that I am today. I guess you could call me Ludington's "Abe Lincoln", although I must confess, unlike Abe, I studied while using" electricity" which undoubtedly helped me obtain an "academic" scholarship to attend college my freshman year. Later I used my many physical talents to obtain a tennis scholarship to finish college

Richard C. Newberg and I's job experience

Exhibit 11 (1 of 2)

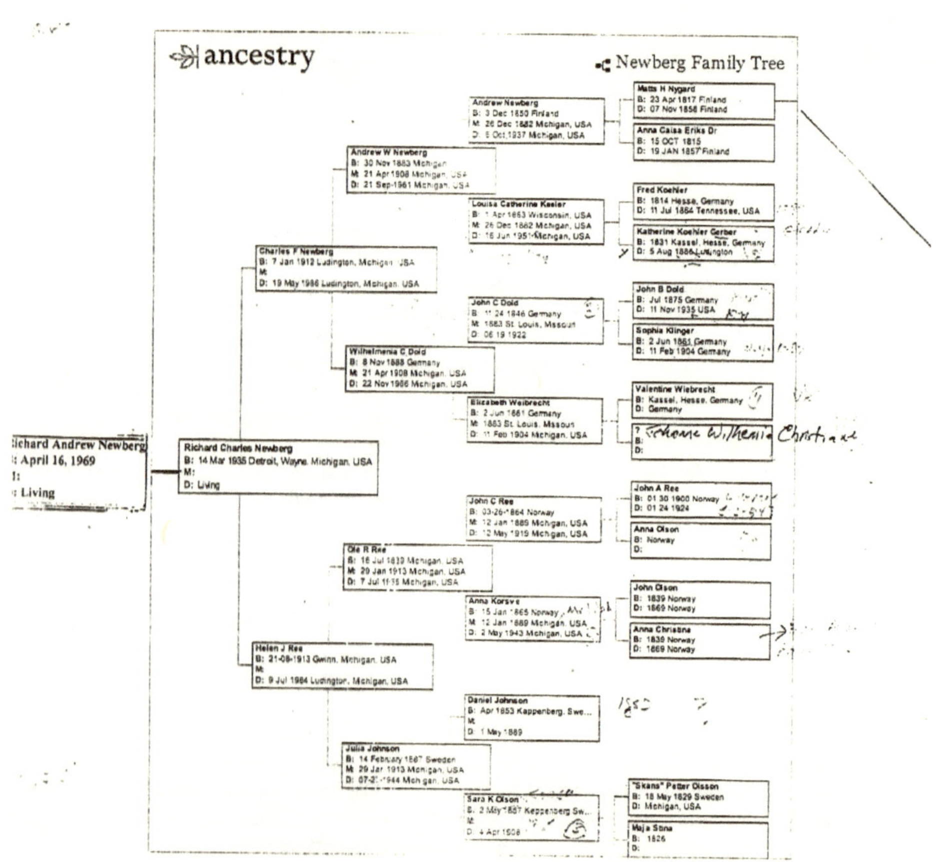

My son and my Ancestry chart

Exhibit 12 (1 of 3)

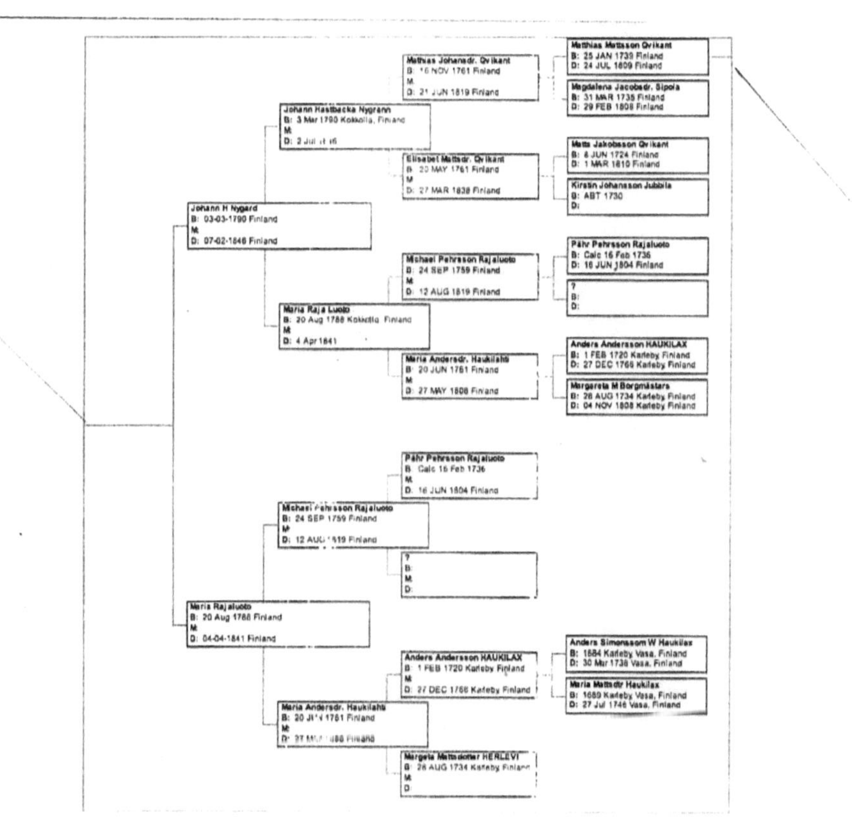

My son and my Ancestry chart

Exhibit 12 (2 of 3)

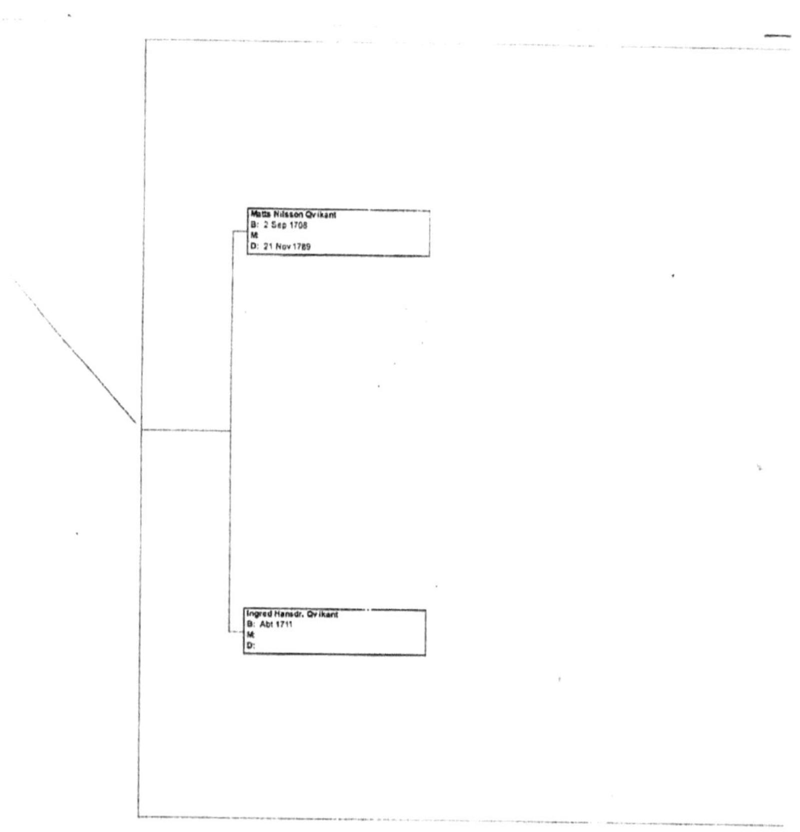

My son and my Ancestry chart

Exhibit 12 (3 of 3)

Fish caught by Paden

Exhibit 13 (1 of 3)

Fish caught by Paden

Exhibit 13 (1 of 3)

Fish caught by Paden (with Cameron's help)

Exhibit 13 (2 of 3)

Family photo of Andrew Newberg, born December 3, 1850

Exhibit 14

Photo of Paden

Exhibit 15

Author's Observation

I would like to personally thank all the "little" people out there who did not encourage me to write this novel and who swore that this attempt at writing would be as bad as my first attempt at writing! It was just this kind of thinking I needed to encourage me to continue.

My mother once told me that everyone has a story in them just waiting to be told. Unlike my first novel that took me 23 years to complete, this "non-fiction" story, just sort of "happened" and kind of wrote itself. It only took me 2 weeks, but it was a full 2 weeks!

Acknowledgements

Regarding the Andys in my life:
I've written this to honor my great-grandfather, Andrew Newberg, from Finland, who helped build and operate the first commercial fishing vessel in and around Ludington, Michigan. I only hope, at 85, that I have accomplished a little of what he did in his 87 years. I thank my co-writer, my son, Andy, for his love and respect for me and his ancestors. Lastly, I thank my best friend, James Anderson, for his humor and for being the best Christian I've ever known.

Regarding the women in my life, I especially thank the following:
My wife Sandy—for her love and devotion every minute of every day. (Happy Birthday one day late to my Halloween birthday girl!) My daughter Juli—for her love and laughter as she drives Miss Daisy-me around and for the enjoyment I get from simply watching her son, Paden, fish. My granddaughter Cameron—for being both the kindest and most generous person I know. My granddaughter Katherine—for always being able to lighten up a room just by entering it. My granddaughter Elizabeth—for being able to dribble a basketball behind her back and through her legs. My daughter-in-law Miguel—for taking my son for a stroll one morning in Epworth and making this book happen! (See note *). Minnie and Julia—for being the kind of grandmothers every boy should have. Honore and her mother, Lois—for helping raise my two kids and for letting me use the kitchen of their house on Lakeshore Drive to watch the sun set on Lake Michigan. My great-aunt Kitty—for making sure I got the oil painting of the *J. H. Rutter* (See note*). My aunt Florence—for those beautiful knitted sweaters she sometimes gave me at Christmas. Virginia—for introducing me to single malt Scotch and, along with Buddy, teaching me about southern hospitality.

*(Special thanks to these women!)

www.ingramcontent.com/pod-product-compliance
Lightning Source LLC
Chambersburg PA
CBHW032125050726
47590CB00008B/2971

* 9 7 8 1 0 8 8 0 7 2 4 2 4 *